IMAGES
of England

THE WIGAN
COALFIELD

The colliery headgear has always been symbolic of the industry as a whole. At Howe Bridge, Atherton the unusual wooden example which gave the colliery the nickname 'Bicycle Pit' dated back to 1879. It is seen here in 1960 after the pit had closed.

IMAGES
of England

THE WIGAN
COALFIELD

Compiled by
Alan Davies
with
Len Hudson ARPS

TEMPUS

First published 1999
Copyright © Alan Davies and Len Hudson, 1999

Tempus Publishing Limited
The Mill, Brimscombe Port,
Stroud, Gloucestershire, GL5 2QG

ISBN 0 7524 1724 X

Typesetting and origination by
Tempus Publishing Limited
Printed in Great Britain by
Midway Clark Printing, Wiltshire

Moss Hall Arley Pit, Ince, c.1905. Wigan's 'Pit Brow Lasses' were employed to carry out manual work on the surface, such as pushing coal tubs to and from the shaft and loading up supplies such as pit props. They became famous enough for a series of tinted postcards to be produced at the turn of the twentieth century. Until 1842 there was every chance they would have been at work below ground, working twelve or even fourteen hours a shift.

Contents

Author Alan Davies, Curator of the Lancashire Mining Museum in Salford.

Acknowledgements

Many thanks to Len Hudson ARPS, Photographic Officer, Wigan Metropolitan Borough Department of Leisure, for skilfully printing the 207 copy photographs.

Special thanks to Tony France for advice with captions and Donald Anderson for access to their collection. Thanks also to the following: John Anderson; Ian Winstanley; Mike Shardlow; Brian Gomm; Vanessa Stott; John Gilman; M.J. Scofield; John Hayworth; Alf Molyneux; William Davies; Frank Berry (Mrs F. Berry); Mrs A. White; Helen Sinclair; P. Hindley; D. Chatfield; Peter Stott; Terry Donnelly; Yvonne Webb and Tony Ashcroft, Wigan Metro Dept of Leisure; Gordon Baron, British Commercial Vehicle Museum, Leyland; The Coal Authority.

Alan Davies,
Lancashire Mining Museum,
City of Salford Education and Leisure Department,
November 1999

Introduction

A visitor to Wigan Metropolitan Borough, created in 1974, cannot imagine how extensive a coalmining industry existed there until recent times. Yet within a four mile radius of the town centre, around 1,100 mine shafts are known to exist, the true figure probably being hundreds more! Twenty-six workable seams are present within the 2,600ft of coal measures rock beneath the town and nearby districts, totalling 85ft of coal. However, geological faults displacing the rocks up to 600m made working the coal difficult.

Wigan can trace, through documents, its coalmining activities as far back as at least 650 years ago and for a brief spell in the late nineteenth century the town was proudly known as 'Coalopolis'.

Mining machinery such as ventilation fans, winding engines, air compressors, pumps and haulage engines were manufactured around Wigan, the products of Worsley Mesnes Ironworks, Woods & Sons or Walker Brothers. The closure of the Bickershaw, Golborne and Parsonage mining complex in 1992 brought to a premature end Wigan's great era of coalmining.

The Early Days

The abundance of timber at the time of the presence of the Roman Legion in the Wigan area could be the reason that coal, being more difficult to obtain, was not fully utilised.

Geologist Edward Hull in his *Coalfields of Great Britain* of 1861 recalled an encounter with supposed 'Roman' workings. Driving a tunnel in the 1850s at Arley to divert the course of the River Douglas, the Arley seam was encountered and found to have been worked in a manner never seen before. This consisted of a series of polygonal chambers interlinked by short passages. Certainly definite Roman workings with polygonal chambers have been found elsewhere in Europe in metalliferous mines.

After the period of the Roman occupation around 410 AD we hear nothing of the working of coal in the area. *Minera carbonum*, probably coal, is mentioned in a document of 1330 held amongst the Arley papers. The land being inherited was at Burnhill, Ashton in Makerfield.

The terms 'Se-cole' and 'Firestone' begin to feature in deeds relating to the Wigan area in 1350. In a land exchange at Shevington between Margaret of Shuttleworth and Robert of Standish, Robert reserved the right to work any 'Fyrston and Secole if it be possible to find them within.'

The term 'Se-cole', from 'sea-coal', derives from the seaborne traffic into London of coal from the north-east and strangely became the general term used for coal wherever found or brought from. Firestone should not be confused with coal, more likely being the fireclay found beneath coal seams, refractory in nature and suitable for firebricks and later on furnaces.

Elsewhere in Wigan, in the fourteenth century, it is known that the Bradshaighs were beginning to realise the potential of the coal beneath their Haigh estate.

The Sixteenth Century and Haigh Cannel

In 1534 an order was made after an action in the Duchy Chancery, Davyd Penington v Squier John Urmeston, 'for dygging and taking Turves and Coles in Westley [Westleigh] in the Countie of Lanc. As also for c'ten wayes and gates for cariage of Turves Coles Corn…'. This authorized Penyngton and other tenants to continue to work coal and peat and transport it to their homes along a set route.

In 1536 an award was made securing the common lands in Hindley and Aspull where 'within late years coal has been found within the said waste and all tenants of Hindley shall henceforth have coal for fuel within their tenements…'

In John Leland's *Itinerary* of 1540 we find: 'Mr Bradeshau hath a place caullid Hawe a myle from Wigan. He hath founde moche Canel like Se Cole in his grounde very profitable to hym. The great Myne of Canale [Cannel coal] is at Hawe two Miles from Wigan. One Bradshaw dwellith at Hawe'. R. Blome, writing in 1680, described it as 'the choicest coal in England'.

In the Duchy court of 1575, four men who had illegally worked Parson Edward Fleetwood's deposits in Whelley Lane, Wigan were fined. In 1595 we find Parson Fleetwood once more complaining of damage to roads in central Wigan, this time citing the mayor and burgesses!

The Seventeenth Century

A colliery was being sunk in 1600 within central Wigan on Ralph Worsley's land. The account of the operation survives including entries for the celebration at reaching coal: 'for drincke and breade at the fyndinge of the coale 12d', 'three mens wages, two days and a half, 3s 2d', 'to John Smethurst for a prop, 3d', 'for three pounds of candles 1s 2d', 'for a rope for the coale pitte 3s 6d.'

In central Wigan, Millgate in 1619 Peter Plat drained his mine into the River Douglas. Plat's workings could be those uncovered in 1960 when the public baths in Library Street were being constructed. Around the 1630's uncontrolled and unsurveyed coalmining became so extensive encroachments into neighbouring workings began to occur, often leading to flooding. Lawsuits followed, forcing some entrepeneurs to drive extensive drainage 'soughs' to enable their mines to have a longer life, without the financial burden of winding water.

In 1652 Sir Rodger Bradshaigh began constructing his 'Great Haigh Sough' of 1,121 yards length, which took seventeen years to complete. The sough was extended in 1853 to 4,600 yards and was still draining working mines in 1929. Bright orange ochreous water still emerges from it today into Bottling Brook.

Records start to appear in the 1670s of individuals being killed by falls of coal at the coalface, explosions, suffocation or even by falling down shafts.

The Eighteenth Century

In his Tour of Great Britain of 1769 Defoe states 'Between Wigan and Bolton is found great plenty of what they call canel or candle coal' (Cannel).

Early Newcomen-type steam engines arrived around 1780, horse gins continuing alongside due to their cheapness. A shaft of 100 to 150 yards depth was about the limit in the Wigan area at this time.

A visitor to Atherton in 1787 stated that,'The coalmines have been long worked; in the deepest part they do not lie more than sixty yards from the surface, they are freed from water by pumps and are not liable to damps [gas]'. At Atherton waterwheel winding was in favour with the Fletchers from the late eighteenth century to the 1830s.

In 1792, Walker's *Tour From London To The Lakes* mentions: 'That excellent coal called cannel is got under the town and in its neighbourhood in great abundance. Besides making the most brilliant fire, this coal is capable of being turned into snuffboxes and many other useful and ornamental toys. Many families have a cannel pit in their back yard and when they are in want of coals they send down a collier who will dig as many in a few hours as will serve the family many months. The pit is then shut up.'

The eighteenth century saw transport of Wigan coal improved firstly by making the River Douglas navigable as far as the Ribble estuary after 1738 and then by the construction of the Leeds & Liverpool Canal from 1791.

Wigan Mining's Great Era – The Nineteenth Century

In 1861, ten per cent of the male population of Wigan (90,000) were employed as miners. In 1863, forty-eight collieries were operating in the Wigan coalfield, raising nearly 4,000,000 tons yearly.

Many mining 'firsts' and major inventions orginated within the Wigan coalfield. The first true coalmining college, Wigan Mining and Mechanical College was founded in 1857. Influential publications such as *The Colliery Manager's Journal* and *The Colliery Guardian*, as well as *The Science and Art of Mining*, aimed at the self-improving workman and mining student, were at one time published in Wigan.

In 1867, Edward Ormerod, engineer at Gibfield Colliery, Atherton designed his safety detaching hook to prevent the miner's cage being overwound, still in use worldwide. The first succesful coalcutting machine was designed in 1869 by J.S. Walker and trialled at Ladies Lane Colliery, Hindley. The first coal washery was developed by Wigan Coal & Iron Co. between 1880 and 1885. The first central mines rescue station serving a number of mines was established in 1908 at Howe Bridge, Atherton. Atherton Collieries were also the first company to provide pithead baths, in 1913 at Howe Bridge Colliery. Parsonage Colliery Leigh, sunk from 1914 to 1920 for many years had the deepest shafts (1,012 yards) and workings in the country.

The Peak Period

Through amalgamations two large companies dominated the Wigan mining industry from the 1870s, Pearson & Knowles Coal & Iron Co. and Wigan Coal & Iron Co.

In 1874 the 558 collieries in Lancashire produced 16,000,000 tons, with Wigan the greatest contributor. The peak year was 1907 when 26,000,000 tons were produced from 200 fewer mines. The increase in productivity can mainly be attributed to mechanization at the coalface, also the best quality seams, some relatively easily accessible were being worked.

'Coal Rush' boomtowns such as Ince and Hindley, Atherton and Tyldesley found their populations swelling dramatically. From 1851 to 1901 Hindley's population shot up from 7,000 to 23,000. The population of Westleigh, Atherton and Tyldesley more than doubled in the same period. In 1901, fifty per cent of male employment in Tyldesley was mining-related.

By 1912 a figure of 31,932 mineworkers (including surface) in the Wigan area is recorded. By 1931, 63.4 per cent of all males aged fourteen and above were employed in mining in Tyldesley.

Decline, Amalgamation and Nationalization

The gradual exhaustion of high quality reserves from the 1920s onwards led to pressure for amalgamations of companies to improve efficiency. The costly legacy of underground water at collieries closed in the early years of the century was seen in 1932 when Wigan Coal Corporation closed it's powerful pumping station at Aspull. Soon after mines to the east at Blackrod and Westhoughton, also south at Rose Bridge, Ince were flooded, some having to close.

To the east of Wigan comprising Leigh, Atherton and Tyldesley the formation of Manchester Collieries in 1929 brought together four coal companies, Astley & Tyldesley Collieries Ltd, Pilkington Colliery Company Ltd, Fletcher Burrows & Co Ltd, and John Speakman & Sons Ltd. Their coal reserves amounted to at least 220 million tons, a fifth of the new company's total reserves.

The coal industry was nationalized in January 1947, with thirty-four mines operating in the Wigan area. They produced 1,299,000 tons but had to raise four tons of water for each ton of coal!

A Sad End

Over 700 million tons of coal has been produced in the Wigan coalfield over the last 600 years. A similar amount still lies below ground. The recent ill-advised rush to wipe out all trace of the British coal industry for highly suspect reasons has temporarily closed the Wigan coal industry. Sadly, thousands of men with the specialist skills peculiar to coalmining built up after long experience found their careers at an end.

It is fitting that one of the finest mining historians this country has ever seen, Donald Anderson, a former Wigan Mine Manager, Mine Surveyor and owner, chose the Wigan coal industry he loved as the subject of his exhaustive researches. Along with former Senior Mines Inspector Jack Lane and Consultant Mining Geologist and Mining Surveyor Tony France, the sheer volume and quality of their work is unparalleled in any other coalfield.

The Photographic Record

Every colliery developed in a unique way with a working life often well over a century. Their surface structures were modified over the years. Each colliery manager had his own preferences as to how he worked the coal measures in his district, giving each pit a unique character. Reading accounts in mining journals or reminiscences leaves the reader new to the subject struggling. Photographs are vital to really understand how Alexandra colliery was laid out at different periods in its life, or how Wigan miners and their families appeared in 1893.

There are some collieries for which not a single photograph has survived. Thousands of images *have* survived though, dating from the 1860s onward. The main collections are to be found at Wigan Metro Dept of Leisure Archives, Leigh, The Lancashire Mining Museum, Salford, and in private collections amassed by Donald Anderson and Tony France, for example. The Revd William Wickham's images held in Wigan Archives, Leigh, of mines and mining communities in Wigan in the late nineteenth century are of national importance.

Selecting 200 photos from over 6,000 means omissions are inevitable due to poor quality or lack of content. I am sorry if this includes a colliery important to you.

One
The Early Days

'Pillar and stall' workings complete with recesses for candles were found during contruction of the public baths in Library Street, Wigan, in 1960. Being close to Millgate, these are likely to be those created by Peter Plat in 1619. Plat was allowed by Bishop Bridgeman, Lord of the Manor, to drain his colliery into the River Douglas, using a channel at the side of Millgate.

Although opencast mining does not receive a good press, it gives a unique insight into ancient methods of working coal mines. Here, the once world famous Haigh Cannel coal has been exposed by the Alexandra opencast site in Whelley, Wigan in August 1989. The pillars of coal were left behind in the mid-eighteenth century to support the workings. Floor lift gradually filled the spaces between these pillars, only to be cleared away again by the opencast contractors. Silver Birch pit props were found amongst the old workings with bark intact, some only four inches in diameter. Areas of coal sooty in appearance tied in with a recorded incident of fire below ground in April 1737. Miners working this coal were known as 'cannellers' and under Wigan Coal & Iron Co. had to wear protective gauze eye shields to protect them from the razor sharp splinters created when working with a hand pick. A number of old Aspull miners alive in the late 1940s bore faces covered with blue scars from working cannel in the 1880s and 1890s.

A coal basket carriage, probably late eighteenth century in date, found in old Orrell Five Feet workings at Dean Wood near Upholland around 1935. After the collier had attached his wooden tally stick to the basket, it was dragged away often by women and children using a harness. The shaft could be hundreds of yards away, the coal being raised to surface by horse gin.

From the Dean Wood old workings, a set of colliers' tools, including a wooden flat bottom spade, a wooden stool used when undercutting the seam, a chisel headed hammer and iron coal wedge for levering the coal down after undercutting. Colliers produced between one and four tons of coal a day at Dean Colliery in 1775 using their own tools, hence the wooden spade. These were left behind possibly after an explosion or fire.

A very rare photograph of a basket winding pit, Winstanley No.5, taken in 1880. Situated north of the M6 near Windy Arbour, the colliery was sunk by Meyrick Bankes in 1856 to two of the best seams, the Orrell 4ft (or Arley) and Orrell 5ft. As late as 1873 all the Winstanley pits wound baskets but the Inspector of Mines demanded that they modernize to cages and tubs due to the danger of men falling out of the basket while travelling the 262yds deep shaft. Winding safety at a shaft such as this relied totally on the experience of the engineman. Monitoring the engine speed and then braking his engine as the baskets approached the surface demanded concentration. When men were being wound any distraction might mean an overwind, the miners being flung over the headgear pulleys.

Surface workers at Rose Bridge Colliery, Ince, in 1865. Wearing heavily reinforced trousers, dust aprons and distinctive headgear, the women pose with their huge shovels and 'riddles' or sieves for grading small coal. This photograph was taken for A.J. Munby, the Cambridge academic who championed working women's causes, in particular that of pit women.

A new colliery being developed – Winstanley Park Pit, around 1900. The shaft was sunk to the Wigan 4ft and 9ft seams. A temporary wooden sinking headgear is being used and a line of small tubs awaits loading from the large 'hoppit' or sinker's bucket. Being within Winstanley Park it was decided to disguise the colliery buildings in the castellated medieval style.

The Revd William Wickham Photographs

The Revd William Arthur Wickham (1849-1929) was born in Wiltshire. Ordained in 1873, his first charge was to be at the Talk O'Th Hill mining village in Staffordshire. His affinity with mining community life brought him to Wigan in 1878 and the next few years found him very busy raising funds for a new St Andrews parish church. Douglas Bank Colliery was visible from the vicarage and around 1891 Wickham gained free access to both the surface and underground at the pit, probably due to the colliery manager being a close friend who often helped out at Sunday bible classes. Only a handful of photographers in the country had attempted to portray life below ground, so the archive of prints and negatives, totalling over 1,000 (which also includes family, local and travel images), in the Wigan collections are of national importance. The following ten images from the Douglas Bank Colliery area, dating from 1891 to 1895, give a taste of the historical importance of William Wickham's work.

Douglas Bank Colliery and the Leeds & Liverpool Canal from the south-west c.1891. The ventilation shaft chimney stands between two wooden headgears. Under Rose Bridge and Douglas Bank Collieries Co. Ltd the shafts reached 500yds intersecting nine workable seams. Although mining ceased in December 1920, the pit was kept open until the early 1930s.

A Douglas Bank collier in 1891 poses obligingly for the vicar. He holds his Davy-type miner's oil lamp in one hand and his water can and 'snap' tin for food in the other. Although probably worn out after a gruelling shift of at least eight hours and desperate to get home, wash and have a nap, he patiently does as he is requested.

Although not working manually during his shift, the undermanager often worked longer hours than the colliers and would end up just as shattered from the travelling of low roads and the high-pressure nature of his work. Handling a tough bunch of Wiganers on piecework in the hostile environment of the pit was not for the weak willed. This man certainly looks up to it!

Five hundred yards below ground, men wait to be signalled off to the surface at Douglas Bank. Cages and guide rods of wire rope had arrived in the late 1830s, replacing basket winding. Cages were designed to carry tubs, the men having to fit it in as best they could! Here five men squeeze in the top deck, the cage fitted with a 'lid' for protection.

At the coalface the collier steadies his shoulder on his knee as he undercuts the face by hand pick. The young lad, aged twelve or fourteen, is using a ratchet and pawl coal drill pinned between roof and floor. After undercutting the coal the shothole drilled by the boy was charged and fired. The collier's sideways posture when undercutting often led to incapacitating eye muscle strain known as nystagmus. In 1891 a Wigan collier could earn 7s a day.

Arguably working harder than coalface workers, the 'drawer' pushed full tubs of a third to half a ton away from the coalface to the main haulage roads. With only the feeble light of his oil lamp he worked in nearly total darkness. The daily battle amongst drawers for empties and supplies often led to fights. In 1891 a Wigan drawer earned 5s 6d a day.

A busy Douglas Bank pit brow. The 'tally lad' is shouting out the collier's number off the tub to the colliery owners' weighman and the miners' 'checkweighman' in the shed. The weight of the tub would indicate if any stone was hidden beneath the coal. After upturning the tub, if this was so, the collier could be fined.

Sheer and abject poverty is evident in this group of miners' children being fed at the Wigan Chief Constables soup kitchen in 1893. The sixteen-week-long Miners Federation of Great Britain strike involved 300,000 miners. It had been called when the coal owners demanded a 25% reduction in wages due to coal price fluctuations. Many Wigan area families lived on soup, potatoes and bread for nearly the whole sixteen weeks. After initially being shocked by the state of Wigan and its inhabitants, which upheld his preconceptions that Wigan was mainly associated with 'bad railway accidents, colliery explosions and monster strikes,' William Wickham was later to say that 'Taking into consideration the perpetual fogs and smoke, the constant floods, the long rows of cottages, the roads which remind one more of swamp tracks rather than of streets of an ancient borough...Well I will tell you that it was your very poverty and lack of beauty which drew my heartstrings to you.' Wickham knew the effect photographs such as this would have on those in positions of influence with a social conscience and is thought to have arranged this group for maximum impact! In fairness some Wigan coal owners and businessmen were already contributing regularly to relief funds. When the strike ended in November the men returned to work on their old terms and a new Concilliation Board was set up with representatives from the mine owners and the miners to negotiate future terms of employment in the hope of avoiding long and costly strikes.

A brief quiet spell at the doctors' surgery, Douglas Bank Colliery 1891. Accidents have always been an accepted daily occurrence in coalmining. Falls of ground at the coalface and in rock tunnels led to wounds and fractures, also serious back injuries. Simple wounds often became infected. Complications would set in leading to death, weeks or sometimes months later.

The 1893 strike. The photographer as ever captures the attention of a crowd of around 120 gathered around an outcrop mine entrance down Platt Lane, near Scholes. Six seams outcropped here in the fields where the disused Whelley Colliery had stood. That colliery had operated a drift mine so locals would be aware of where coal seams lay in the area.

A group of Wigan colliery surface workers, or pit brow girls, *c*.1895. James Millard, who had a studio in Market Street (where the Queens Hall is today), produced this superb image as a souvenir card. He was a man of many talents, building his own studio and also sculpting statues of a pit brow girl and mill girl to stand outside his business. After the Coal Mines Act of 1842, women and girls were banned from work below ground. Many found employment on the surface, working in the screening sheds grading coal, picking out dirt from the coal or loading supplies such as pit props into tubs for use below ground. For many years Lancashire had more women working on the pit brow than any other coalfield. Distinctive styles of dress developed at individual collieries. One can only guess at the colours that may have been present in this scene. The interest taken in the welfare of pit women through the work of Cambridge academic A.J. Munby (1828-1910), who had studied particularly the Wigan area pit women since the late 1850s, led to wider knowledge of their working lives. Parliament attempted to halt their work in 1887 and 1911, thwarted by successful protests and deputations to London by the women and girls themselves. By the mid-1950s only two Lancashire collieries employed pit brow women. The last ever Lancashire pit brow woman left Golborne Colliery in 1966 and the last in the country finished at Whitehaven in 1972.

Two
The Aspull Area

The Great Haigh Sough which drained Sir Roger Bradshaigh's Cannel workings. For 1652 this was a massive undertaking. The first 1,121yds, from Bottling Wood to Park Pit to the north, took seventeen years to drive. No one had ever photographed or filmed within the sough until 1991, when mine explorers using gas detectors, mine safety lamps and rescue breathing apparatus found the tunnel in good condition, although a claustrophobic experience! After approximately 200yds, increasing amounts of hardened ochre and eventually the lack of oxygen forced an end to the venture.

Bradshaigh Sough, 1991. Standing inside Cannel Hollows shaft with the sough access below. This shaft was sunk around 1653 and is approximately 5ft in diameter and 24ft deep, of stone blocks with ladder supports. Shafts like this allowed material to be raised to surface and ventilation to take place and were welcome relief from the cramped conditions in the sough, 3ft high at best in this section. We can only wonder at the type of man who could endure such cramped working conditions. 'Soughers', as they were called (a Soughers Lane exists near Ashton In Makerfield), were highly paid and often rewarded with large amounts of beer or spirits! The Great Haigh Sough was extended in 1676-1866, eventually reaching Aspull Pumping Pit, a distance of 4,600yds. It was last officially travelled in 1923 when over 300 gallons per minute flowed out. The 1991 explorers only managed an hour at a time due to fatigue and the oppressive atmosphere of the confined space. The sough is now grilled off and visitors should keep well away even from the entrance as suffocating air and explosive gas still flow out.

Meadow Pit, Aspull, c.1895. William Pit is in the distance. A French mining engineer visiting Aspull in 1901 stated that 'The frail limbs and childlike faces of some of them indicate that only light work could humanely be asked of them, so that concentration plays a greater part in their work than muscular effor.' The strong, fit girls seen here perhaps felt differently!

Meadow Pit, *c.*1910. This pit was first worked around 1780 to work the cannel seam, then closed and filled up around 1800. In 1851 it was reopened and sunk to the Arley seam at 947ft, producing 60,000 tons of coal a year by the 1860s. William Pit nearby served as the ventilation shaft. In 1924, 462 men were employed below ground and ninety-nine on the surface. The colliery closed in May 1927.

Alexandra Pit, left, and Lindsay No.3 Pit, *c.*1908. The first pits on this site were the three Lindsay pits of 12ft diameter sunk in 1856. Loco *Manton* can be seen, newly built at Kirkless workshops. The headgear at Alexandra had to support a total cages and guide rope weight of seventy-two tons, winding 800 tons per shift at the time of the photograph. The pit was named after Princess Alexandra, who with the Prince of Wales stayed at Haigh in 1873, the year sinking began to the Pemberton series of seams. It was later deepened in 1887 to the Arley at 772yds. The colliery employed 370 miners and 103 surface workers in 1905. It closed in June 1955 with its workforce down to 189.

Alexandra Pit, 1911. Shortly after the previous photograph was taken, the colliery headgear collapsed after a failure in the shaft structure. This was a very rare occurrence and certainly not due to the headgear being poorly designed. Note the massive dimensions of the timbers, of Scandinavian pitch pine clamped together with iron straps.

Jim Sharrock, winding engineman at Alexandra Pit, c.1910. The steam engine at Alexandra arrived in 1876, built by Yates of Blackburn and costing £2,830. Cylinders were 35in diameter by 78in stroke. Jim (1895-1986) played Rugby League as a full-back for Wigan and England, making 233 appearances with 117 tries and 7 goals.

Scot Lane Moor Pit No.5 was a familiar part of the landscape in this 1920s scene, when 'Walking Day' was in full flow. A Wigan Coal & Iron Co mine, it closed in 1924. It had employed 329 miners and sixty-eight surface workers, who were redeployed to Meadow Pit and Crawford Pit, which then accessed the colliery's reserves.

The imposing surface layout of Crawford Pit, Aspull, around 1908. This was one of Wigan Coal & Iron's 'show pits'. A central engine house contained two vertical steam winders serving both shafts, sunk in the 1840s. No.1 accessed the Bone at 223yds and No.2 the Arley seam at 318yds. The pit closed in 1928 at which point 251 people were employed below ground and fifty-nine on the surface.

WIGAN COAL & IRON Co.,
LIMITED.

NOTICE TO

COLLIERS

1.—When a tub gets off the road, the person lifting it on must not get hold of the buffer to do so, but must get hold of the coupling or the bottom of the tub.

2.—In addition to the direction given in Special Rule 47, as to securing his working place, every collier or other workperson whose duty it is to set props to support the roof, must set them at distances from the face and from each other which will in no case exceed the distance from one another specified by the management for the particular mine in which he is working, and must be set nearer where necessary.

3.—Sprags must be set by the collier or other person holing, not further than 4ft. apart, and must be renewed in the event of their becoming unsafe.

4.—No canneller is allowed to use his pick at the face unless he has his eyes protected with a wire gauze shield, or other suitable appliance provided by the Company.

5.—Before any person commences to pull ley, coal, roof, or sides, in any working place or road, he shall see that there is no prop or anything else to prevent him stepping out of the way of such ley, coal, roof, or sides when it falls.

6.—When two or more men are working together, each must be careful to be out of the swing of the other's pick.

Strowger & Son, Printers, Wigan.

One of a series of safety notices issued to employees of Wigan Coal & Iron, c.1910. Item 4 relates to the nature of cannel coal, which when worked with a hand pick created thin and very sharp splinters. A recent serious accident such as the loss of an eye is probably the reason for the inclusion of item 6.

Three
Standish Area Mines

Miners run off to the baths at Victoria Colliery, Standish in March 1946. Two shafts of 20ft diameter were sunk in 1900 by Wigan Coal & Iron Co. Eighteen seams were accessed including the famous Arley coal, but in a heavily faulted area. The colliery often struggled to make a profit, its workforce of 434 finally losing their jobs in May 1959. Note the magnificent engine house behind which served both shafts. No.1 Pit is seen in the distance with its substantial wooden headgear.

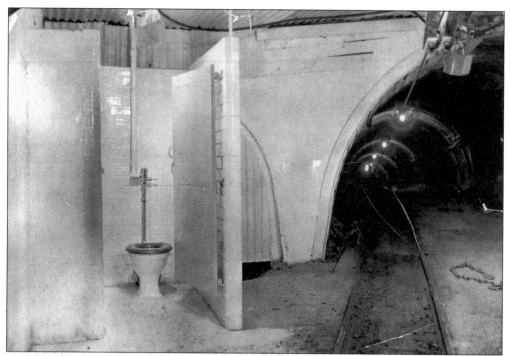

North Pit bottom at Victoria Pit in 1948. A rare sight down a coal mine and obviously worthy of a photograph was this pristine toilet. Experiments with underground toilets over the years were never really successful, with cleaning problems and a distinct lack of men keen to service them! Generally miners regarded most places underground as sufficing for a toilet.

Taylor Pit No.1, Standish, near Birley Wood, c. late 1950s. The 16ft diameter pulley wheel enabled flat rope winding to be used. The pit was sunk in the early 1860s to the Arley seam at 489yds. Named after John Tayleur who secured the lease from the Standish Coal Co in 1844. It closed in the late 1920s but was retained for pumping, washing and ventilation purposes until 1954.

The 16in-square timber baulks of Giants Hall No.3 pit headgear. A Haigh Foundry engine wound to a depth of 616yds using flat ropes. These stretched during the shift forcing the engineman to have to bank the cages manually as they approached the surface. The colliery closed in January 1961 with over 400 miners having been employed.

Giants Hall Colliery, c. early 1930s, from the north-east. Sunk in 1875, eleven seams including the Arley at 608yds were accessed. This view shows the offices and workshops in the foreground. The square ventilation chimney drew air from No.2 pit to the left. A healthy crop standing in one of Giants Hall Farm's fields indicates the rural setting of the pit.

A late 1930s photograph inside the women's section of the pithead baths at Chisnall Hall Colliery, opened in 1934. The women, after a shift in the screen sheds, are washing the pit dirt out of their hair. Parsonage Colliery at Leigh also provided such facilities. In 1938 approximately 1,300 women were working on the surface at Lancashire coal mines.

Chisnall Hall Colliery, Coppul Moor in the late 1930s, looking west. Formerly under Pearson & Knowles, amalgamation into the Wigan Coal Corporation took place in 1930, when the colliery employed 723 men below ground and 158 on the surface. Around the time of the photograph, the colliery was producing over 300,000 tons of coal per year.

This unusual view of 10 June 1951 shows the changeover from wooden to steel girder headgear at Chisnall Hall No.1 pit (the ventilation shaft). This was accomplished without interrupting winding operations by building the new headgear around the existing one. Note the surface tub circuit with 'creeper' to pull the tubs up the incline by their axles.

Demolition of the chimney at Chisnall Hall, with No.1 pit behind. One of the last of the larger Wigan area collieries, the National Coal Board announced its closure in March 1967. In its final year 222,278 tons of coal were wound with a workforce of 617. They were taken on at collieries such as Bickershaw, Golborne, Parsonage and the newly developing Parkside.

Elnup Wood's silver birches frame the impressive entrance to Standish Hall drift mine, *c*.1950. A 'run' of mine cars has just been hauled to surface. After nationalization in 1947, the NCB decided to access small areas of coal reserves via drifts, including Standish Hall from December 1948. The mine accessed the Ince 4ft and 7ft seams and was finally exhausted by July 1961.

This view looking south *c*.1953 shows Welch Whittle Colliery, Coppull, with Chisnall Hall Colliery tip behind. The first Welch Whittle Colliery, sunk by John Darlington and dating back to around 1855, was closed in 1880. The Blainscough Colliery Co. Ltd reopened it in 1894. It closed in February 1960 when its British Railways contract for steam-raising coal ended.

Tom Smith, colliery surveyor, and David Owen, surveyor's linesman, enjoy a brief spell of sunshine before surveying down Welch Whittle Colliery in 1950. This was carried out using a miner's dial, a large diameter tripod-mounted compass with sighting arms. Miners at the coalface handfilled an impressive 100,000 tons at Welch Whittle in 1950.

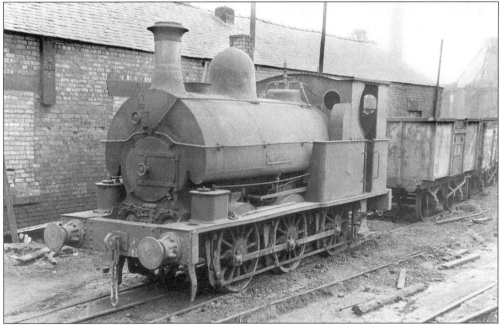

Built by Nasmyth Wilson, Manchester, in 1898, 0-6-0 ST locomotive *Wantage* is seen at Welch Whittle Colliery in October 1957. One of Wigan Coal and Iron's, later Wigan Coal Corporation's, stock, this loco had worked at John Pit Standish. Named after Lord Wantage, an earlier director of Wigan Coal and Iron Co, it was scrapped in May 1958 at Kirkless workshops.

Ellerbeck Colliery pit bank in the mid-1950s, featuring Banksman 'Ronnie'. At collieries winding tubs, pit bank workers, the winder and the pit bottom men virtually never had a breather. Situated between Coppull and Adlington, the colliery employed 216 miners and forty-eight men on the surface in 1955, raising around 3,000 tons a week.

Hilton House and Red Moss Coal Co. Ltd sank Ellerbeck Colliery's shafts around 1875. This photograph was taken soon after reorganization in 1958-1959. Until then, not even electric lighting or pithead baths had been on site. It closed three times: in 1928-1929, 1932 and finally in August 1965, with most of the 220 men finding work at the recently opened Parkside Colliery, Newton.

Four
Around Pemberton and Orrell

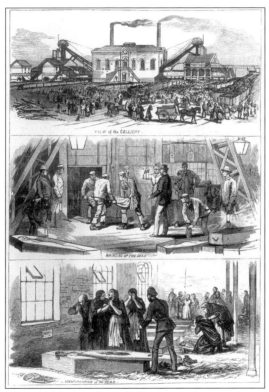

The *Illustrated London News*, 20 October 1877. A full page engraving depicting scenes at Pemberton Colliery after the explosion of the eleventh in the Wigan Nine Feet seam workings. Thirty-six men died, including the colliery manager and two undermanagers after attempting a rescue operation. Identification of the men in the temporary mortuary is seen taking place in the lower illustration. This was often only possible by their boots, teeth or scraps of clothing. Large explosions and disasters occurred fairly regularly from the 1840s through to the First World War period. Not until 1908-1909 did the coalowners and mining engineers make concerted efforts to ascertain the influence coal dust had in major explosions, publishing their findings in 1910. In the very same year at Pretoria Colliery, Atherton, the third largest disaster in British coalmining history occurred, with 344 killed. A gas ignition followed by a full-blown coal dust explosion was the cause.

King Pit steam winding engine at Pemberton Colliery. Made by Haigh Foundry in 1870 and costing £3,500, this had two cylinders of 36in diameter and 72in stroke. Using Cornish valves, link motion and two fast eccentrics for each cylinder, its drum of 19ft 4in could wind $7\frac{1}{2}$ tons of coal 520yds up the shaft in thirty-nine seconds!

Pemberton Colliery pit brow women, c.1905. Visitors to Wigan found it fascinating that women were working on the pit brows, wearing distinctive outfits and wielding picks, riddles and shovels and were prepared to pay for specially produced cards available at Mr Millard's shop and studio (where the Queens Hall, Wigan, stands today).

EXHIBITING

COAL

COKE

BRICKS

DRAIN
TILES

CREOSOTE
OIL

&c.

PILLARS OF LOCAL INDUSTRY

PEMBERTON COLLIERY C.º (1929) LTD
WIGAN

PEMBERTON
COLLIERY C.º
(1929) LTD.

PHONE
74
PEMBERTON

EXHIBITING

COAL

COKE

BRICKS

DRAIN
TILES

CREOSOTE
OIL

&c.

WIGAN CARNIVAL, JULY 11.ᵗʰ 1931.-"PILLARS OF LOCAL INDUSTRY"
FIRST PRIZE · TRADES EXHIBIT SECTION ·

The labeling says it all! A prizewinning display mounted on a Leyland Model TA Badger truck. Pemberton Colliery Co. extracted the maximum available from the coal and fireclay it mined, operating a large coke and by-products works, producing tar, benzol and creosote. A brick and tile works was also in operation.

PEMBERTON COLLIERY SCHOOL R.F.C.
WIGAN LEAGUE CHAMPIONS 1911-12. SALTER & SALTER SHIELD WINNERS 1912.

1912.

Another victorious season for Pemberton Colliery School rugby team. The teacher to the right is George Millard, son of the Wigan photographer. George stated that many of his pupils were part-timers, working at nearby May Mill from 5.30 a.m. until dinnertime. Coming to school in the afternoon they would often fall asleep on their desks, to be woken again with the cane!

Pony 'tenter' Jim Downham in the Wigan 5ft stables at Pemberton Colliery around the early 1940s. Nearly 300 yards below ground Jim chalks on the board details of ponies, where they were working or which ones were being shoed. Pemberton was the last Lancashire colliery to use pony 'putting' extensively, with nearly 250 in use. A ready supply of mice kept the cat very busy!

Old style timber headgears, raised pit bank and coal heap at Orrell or Walthew House Colliery, c.1920. Sunk in 1846 by J M Hustler and Co., this was situated at Marsh Green, off Walthew House Lane and to the west of Douglas Bank Colliery. Eventually sunk to the Smith seam at 439 yards, it closed in 1924 with the loss of 235 miners and 103 surface workers jobs.

Previous pages: Blundell's Pemberton Colliery, October 1931. From left to right: Queen Pit, King Pit, Prince Pit and the old Bye Pit. It was sunk from 1815 to 1827, later reaching the Orrell 4ft seam at 633 yards. In 1931, 1,365 miners and 473 surface workers were employed and the company owned nearly 2,000 railway wagons. Production ceased in November 1946.

Five
Billinge Area Collieries

A few hundred yards south-west of Billinge opposite Birchley Wood stood Birchley Colliery. Around 1910 we see the surface workmen, dog, carthorse and probably the owner on the right. The surface layout is of an older type, small, single-shaft colliery, with a raized wooden 'heapstead' structure. This allowed overhead screening of coal straight from tubs into the waiting cart. The small damaged tub in the foreground looks to be around 2 or 3 cwt capacity. The colliery worked the high quality Orrell Five Foot or Rushy Park seam for local household use. Operated by William Hilton from around 1890, then Hitchen and Moss, it closed in 1919. Twenty-five miners and eleven surface workmen had been employed.

Brown Heath Colliery was situated a quarter of a mile north-east of Carr Mill Dam. Here, around 1912, colliers pose with their handtools andshaftsinkers with their compressed air rock drills. The shaftsmen are wearing waterproof capes and Sou' Westers. Operated by Billinge Collieries Ltd, 117 miners and sixty surface workmen were employed in its final year in 1926.

Gauntley No.1 Pit, west of Billinge Hospital, was sunk around 1894 by W Hilton. Forty-four miners were working the Middle Mountain seam and fireclay on closure in 1967. Its wooden headgear, seen here after closure, was the last in the Lancashire coalfield. Dismantled in 1978 andthen re-erected at Haigh Hall, it now awaits restoration at Astley Green Colliery museum.

Manager, surveyor, mineowner and mining historian Donald Anderson (second on the right) had worked in South African gold mines, later managing an Indian coalmine. He opened Dalton Lees Coal and Fireclay drift near Parbold in 1942, then Quaker House Colliery in 1947. Here in 1978 he says farewell to underground haulage engineman Jim Mullineux at Quaker House.

Empties wait to go back down the drift (top right) at Quaker House Colliery in 1982. Thirty miners and thirteen surface workmen were employed at the time of the photograph. The company also operated Leyland Green Drift Mine a few hundred yards to the south, with eight miners and two surface workmen. Quaker House Colliery closed in 1992 after forty-five years of production.

Windy Arbour Colliery in 1980 after closure. Formerly Winstanley No.4 pit, it was sunk by Meyrick Bankes in 1837. Windy Arbour Colliery Co. Ltd worked the pit from the early 1920s. Soon after nationalization in 1947, 105 miners and thirty-eight surface workers were employed, making it one of the largest licensed mines in the country. It closed in 1977, then operated on a small scale until 1979.

The Windy Arbour site has been opencast mined three times, 1950-1952, 1983 and 1999. St Helens College mining students are seen visiting the site in October 1983 under the expert guidance of lecturer Alistair Macmillan. A cross section of an old road in the King seam is being studied. The seam is at the base of the photograph, the strata slowly cratering upwards.

The last mine to be opened near Billinge, to the north, was Castle Mine Drift, owned by Castle Mines, Ipswich. Here, in September 1983, the tubs have arrived at this short-lived mine. Working the Orrell Yard, seam conditions were tough at the face with a poor roof and water to deal with. Faceworkers had to wear waterproofs while handfilling coal onto a conveyor.

Castle Mine again in 1983, the drift being laid out on the surface. Driving this was to be difficult, passing through an old opencast infill. By 1987, twenty-three miners and six surface workers were employed, producing coal for power station use. The mine had closed by 1990.

Walker Bros. (Wigan), Ltd.
Engineers, Wigan

TELEGRAMS—"Pagefield, Wigan"
CODES—Lieber, ABC, A1, Moreing & Neale's Mining, and Western Union

PATENT AIR COMPRESSORS
355,000 I.H.P. AT WORK

IN GREAT BRITAIN, FRANCE, GERMANY, AUSTRIA, SPAIN, RUSSIA, HOLLAND, CANADA, SOUTH AMERICA, INDIA, JAPAN, SOUTH AFRICA, CHINA, AUSTRALIA, NEW ZEALAND, &c. &c.

WALKER VENTILATING FANS
("INDESTRUCTIBLE" TYPE)

CAPACITY OF INSTALLATIONS NOW AT WORK OR ON ORDER **EXCEEDS 50,000,000 FEET PER MINUTE**

Above and below: Two advertizements from the 1920s. Absolutely everything a colliery and its workforce needed could be provided by Wigan area companies, from a pit headgear to miners' oil lamps, from coal sacks to the famous miners' toffees, 'Uncle Joes Mint Balls!'

PEPPER MILL BRASS FOUNDRY CO.,

Colliery

Winding

Indicators.

Telegrams
Pepper, Wigan.

Engine and Boiler Fittings of all descriptions, Castings in Brass, Gun Metal, and Phosphor Bronze. Estimates and Specifications free.

Telephone No. 19.

WIGAN.

Six
The Hindley and Ince Area

The *Illustrated London News* regularly sent out artists to cover the scene after large colliery disasters, this time at the Arley pit of Ince Hall Coal and Cannel Co. This engraving was published in the 9 April 1853 issue andwas a view from the south-east of Wigan town centre, east of Britannia Bridge, with the distinctive tower of All Saints church visible. St Catherines church and Birkett Bank can be seen to the right. An explosion had occurred in the Arley pit on 24 March, killing fifty-eight men and boys. A further explosion at another of the company's nearby mines a year later resulted in eighty-nine deaths. The Inspector of Mines, Joseph Dickinson, severely criticized the company's lack of managerial discipline in enforcing safe working practices in obviously gassy pits. The engraving shows the two wooden headgears atop the shafts of 414yds depth. A central vertical steam winder is in operation and a glimpse of the mast of a boat on the Leeds & Liverpool Canal can be seen behind the tub tramroad to the left. The colliery had two docks and a saw-pit in that area. Ince Hall Colliery had closed its Arley and Yard seam workings by 1895 and 1898.

This superb record of around 1900 shows two eras of Hindley life, the pre-industrial thatched cottages and the wooden headgear of Ladies Lane Colliery. Thomas Gidlow sank the colliery in 1857. In 1871 he sold out to Wigan Coal and Iron Company for £32,000. Closure of the colliery's King and Yard seams came in 1907 and 1908.

Just a few mouths to feed here in November 1893 for the Lower Ince Central Relief Fund! That year, 300,000 miners nationally reacted to a proposed 25% cut in wages by striking for sixteen weeks. The strike ended in November, so the photograph was probably taken as a record after the great victory, won through enormous hardship.

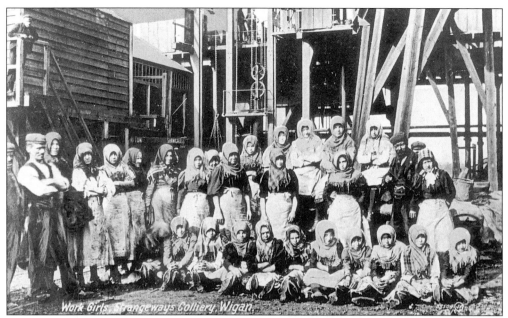

Women working on the pit brow, especially around Wigan, Hindley and Atherton, attracted a great deal of interest. This tinted postcard view from around 1906 shows twenty-five employed at Strangeways Hall Colliery, Low Green, owned by Crompton and Shawcross. The pit was situated half a mile south-west of the Bird I'Th Hand pub, Hindley.

Strangeways Hall Colliery. Pit brow women stand on the timber heapstead. Neatly stacked pit props await use underground. This tinted postcard from around 1906 is a wider version of the previous one. An old colliery, dating back to around 1842 under Byrom, Taylor and Byrom, it closed in 1937. At the time of the postcard 390 miners and 181 surface workers were employed.

The only photograph known of Swan Lane Colliery, probably on closure in 1927. It was sunk around 1864 by John Johnson. The colliery accessed the LNWR near Hindley Green Station and the branch line is seen crossing the lane. Closure came firstly in 1910, followed by reopening under Swan Lane Collieries Ltd, then finally in 1927 with 384 miners and ninety-nine surface workers losing their jobs.

Grange Colliery, c.1920s. Sunk around the late 1890s by Crompton and Shawcross, the mine was situated half a mile down and to the west of Park Road. This view south-east is probably from the footpath which headed from near Hindley and Abram Grammar School to Hindley and Platt Bridge Station. Note the stacks of pit props alongside the sidings.

A frightening bunch of Grange Colliery miners and surface staff, especially the front row! The colliery was relatively short-lived and this was possibly taken after closure had been announced in 1927. Grange Colliery had employed over 400 miners and eighty surface workers in 1924.

Though only a distant view, this 1920s photograph is the only one known to be in existence of Hindley Field Colliery, seen here from the Bickershaw Lane Bridge over the LMSR. The pit was sunk around 1865 by Norris, Richards and Co. To the right is Hindley Field House, with California Pit dirt heaps behind. The colliery closed in 1927 with the loss of 350 miners' and ninety-nine surface workers' jobs.

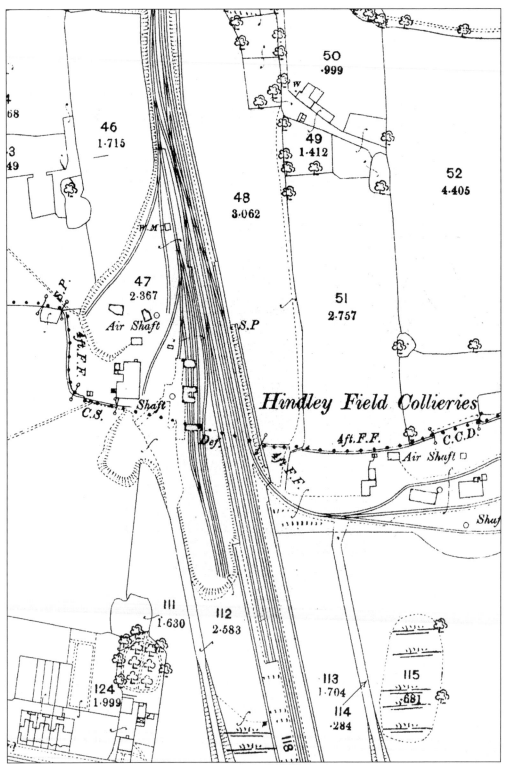

Hindley Field Colliery shown on the 1901 edition Ordnance Survey 6in map.

Seven
Ince, Platt Bridge, Garswood and Abram

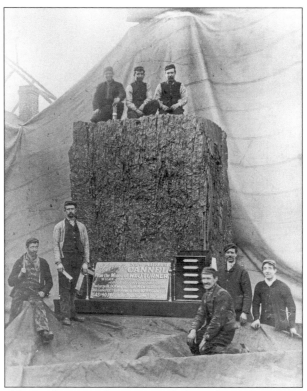

An 11 ton 14cwt block of 'New Abram Cannel' bound for the International Exhibition, Chicago in 1893, from Wigan Junction Colliery. Wigan Cannel was exported to France, Italy and America in the late eighteenth and early nineteenth centuries. To work around and extract a block of cannel this size without breakage was a testament to the skills of the miners. The cannel present at Wigan Junction Colliery was not the same deposit as at Haigh. It lay at a depth of 400yds beneath the 1ft-thick Wigan Four Foot coal and had a section of 5ft 10in. Workings in the cannel were abandoned in March 1920. The colliery was situated north of Park Lane, Abram, a quarter of a mile to the north of Maypole Colliery, where the present day industrial estate operates. Sunk in 1875 by William and John Turner, it became a subsidiary of Pearson & Knowles Coal & Iron Co. in 1907, then from 1930 to 1946 part of the Wigan Coal Corporation. Nationalized in 1947, it closed in 1962.

The date is 18 November 1939. Even though other more pressing thoughts and worries must have been in their minds this happy and stylish looking group of ladies smile for the cameraman. They are attending the opening ceremony of the women's section of the new pithead baths at Wigan Junction Colliery. The building with its water tower still stands today.

Taken around 1939, this photograph shows a fine example of herringbone or cockering timbering, 200 yards below ground in the Ince 4ft seam at Wigan Junction Colliery. This method was resorted to when the roadway sides were strong but the roof needed support. Roads supported in this way often stood for generations.

Inside 'C' Air Raid Shelter at Wigan Junction Colliery during the Second World War. The Wigan area and its coal mines were well known to the Germans when in 1942 they sent reconnaissance planes to photograph industrial sites in the north-west. The area avoided being seriously targeted though, being roughly midway between Liverpool and Manchester.

Captioned 'Snow Week 1940' Wigan Junction. A severe spell of weather in January left snow on the ground for a month with drifts up to six feet deep. The wartime coal shortage meant searching for useable coal on the dirt tips, probably for internal use, was a necessity. At least by now the new baths and cosy canteen were available to recover in afterwards!

Wigan Junction Colliery No.4 downcast shaft stands behind this group of Bevin Boys, c.1945. After the outbreak of the Second World War, the Mines Department stated that it needed an additional 40,000 young men to replace those who had left to join the forces or work elsewhere. Colliery workers aged eighteen, twenty-one, twenty-five and thirty were not allowed to leave the industry which became a reserved occupation. By 1943 the manpower and output situation was serious. Ernest Bevin, Minister of Labour and National Service, decided that men aged between eighteen and twenty-five would be selected by ballot to be conscripted into the coal industry. By September 1943, 13,078 either opted for or volunteered to go into coal mining. This was not enough though and further measures were taken to boost the workforce. By late 1945, 5,900 conscripts and 7,200 'optants' were at work in the mines. The end of hostilities in 1945 did not mean the 'Bevin Boys' could immediately leave and many continued working well into 1946, others making a career in the industry.

Timber pit props and private owner wagons take up every available space in the sidings at Abram Colliery, c.1928. Nos 1 and 2 pits are in the distance viewed from Nos 4 and 5 pits to the south. Sunk around 1873 by Heyes and Johnson and eventually reaching the Arley seam at 650 yards, closure and amalgamation with Ackers Whitley came in 1933, leading to the creation of Bickershaw Collieries Ltd. Just before closure, 700 miners and 186 surface workers were employed.

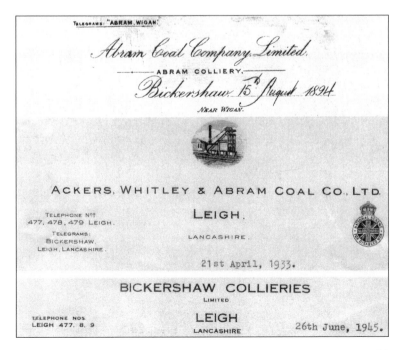

Company letterheads.

Seventy-five men and boys died when an explosion occurred in the Wigan Four Feet workings at Maypole Colliery on Tuesday 18 August 1908. The *Illustrated London News* devoted a full page of early examples of 'reportage' photography, on the spot records of the events soon after the disaster. A few years earlier an artist would have been dispatched to the colliery, working up engravings afterwards.

60

About a week after the explosion at Maypole Colliery, the extent of the damage even on the surface can be seen, with the blown off roof of the ventilation fan house to the left. There are also gaps in the timber cladding of the normally airtight No.1 upcast shaft headgear nearby. Some of the colliery buildings still stand today as part of the Maypole Industrial Estate.

A scene repeated many times over the centuries in mining districts. Relatives and probably wives of men still below ground await news. Sadly, these very women were soon to receive the news they all dreaded. By this time the only three men to survive had already been rescued. One body had also been brought out. The date was probably 18 August 1908.

18 August, the day of the explosion. The explosion occurred at 5.10 p.m. so we are probably looking at most of the day shift men who had finished work shortly after 4 p.m. and rushed back on hearing the blast.

THE ONLY SURVIVORS OF THE DISASTER AT THE MAYPOLE COLLIERY, ABRAM, AUGUST 18TH, 1908.

Will Smith Series, Wigan.
Copyright.

EDWARD FARRELL, 3, CAMBRIDGE ST., WIGAN.   WM. DORAN, 5, HARDYBUTTS, WIGAN.   RICHARD FAIRHURST, 11, CROWN STREET, HINDLEY.

These three men survived the Maypole explosion, working in a different seam to the other seventy-five men and boys, the Bickershaw 7ft. William Doran of 5 Hardybutts, Wigan, (centre) stated, 'I was knocked down by the force of the explosion and fell face forward. We tried to travel along the road towards the pit eye, but all the lights went out except one and we were afraid to go on. We decided to await events in a manhole. After remaining for some time we were eventually reached by the rescue party who conducted us from underground by another shaft'. (Wigan Junction Colliery).

No pithead baths to head off to here at Mains Colliery, Bamfurlong, c.1906. Situated half a mile west of Dover Bridge on the Leeds & Liverpool Canal, the colliery probably dated back to the late 1840s. Cross Tetley & Co. Ltd owned it from 1866 to 1934, Wigan Coal Corporation from 1934 to 1946, then the National Coal Board until its closure in 1960.

Wooden headgears above Mains Colliery No.1 downcast shaft (nearest) with No.2 upcast behind, in this view of around 1910. No.1 was sunk 365 yards to the Wigan Four Foot seam. Amazingly, the saddle tank loco has stumped even the top railway experts as regards identification but is thought to be of Scottish origin.

The new Ince 6ft and King seam drift mine at Mains Colliery being developed in May 1957. The 6ft was also known as the Ince Furnace seam, containing 4ft 7in of coal split by a 2ft-thick dirt band. Mains closed in September 1960, with the loss of 467 miners' and 110 surface workers' jobs. The site has now been extensively landscaped.

No less than seventy-three similarly costumed pit brow women can be seen in this superb record from around 1910 of Ince Moss Colliery No.4 Pit, owned at the time by Pearson and Knowles Coal and Iron Co. The screening sheds stand behind to the left while the materials tub hoist is behind the higher group of women.

This roadway to the coalfaces looks relatively modern, with the coal conveyor and two-piece steel rings for support, yet is titled 'Ince Moss 29.4.1938'. Those with keen eyesight will notice the men's handpicks, shovels and hammers stacked to the right. Note the timber lagging boards above the steel arches, already suffering from roof pressure a week after being set.

Ince Moss, c.1936. Just visible is Pearson's Flash, created after subsidence. Central is the engine house and chimney of No.6 Pit, to the right Nos 4 and 3 Pits. Sunk from 1863 onwards, it came under Wigan Coal Corporation from 1930 to 1946, then the NCB, closing in 1962. 358 miners and 194 surface workers were employed in the final year.

Industrial locomotive photographers often included the collieries the locomotives worked at. Not for this locomotive some exotic name, simply *No.1*, seen at Ince Moss No.6 in 1956. Purchased in 1900 by Pearson and Knowles, the 0-6-0 saddle tank was supplied by the famous Robert Stephenson & Co. Ltd, Newcastle and Darlington.

Low Hall Colliery, Platt Bridge. No.7 New Zealand shaft collapsed on 30 April 1945. Loco *Dorothy*, driver Loudovic Berry and thirteen loaded coal wagons were swallowed up as the shaft filling gave way beneath the railway line. With difficulty the shaft can be made out top left along with one of the loco buffers under the rail.

Driver Berry on the footplate of loco *Dorothy* in the late 1920s. If ever an incident could be described as unique in a national sense relating to the Wigan area coalfields and their history, the tragic incident involving this locomotive and its driver must be the case. Over the years since the incident, many versions of the places and events involved have been created. Now is the chance to give the true course of events. The Moss Hall Coal Co. Ltd purchased locomotive *Dorothy*, a Class X2 six coupled wheel, internal cylinder saddle tank, in 1908 from Peckett & Sons of Bristol. Locomotives operated from the company's Low Hall Colliery engine shed. Driver Loudovic Berry's father was a colliery engine driver and he wished for no other employment. On 30 April 1945 *Dorothy*, with driver Loudovic Berry in control, was shunting a train of thirteen loaded wagons near Brookside when the ground beneath the line cratered and collapsed. Brakesman John Ward signalled to Loudovic, who immediately applied the brakes but to no avail. The last wagon entered the crater, pulling the rest of the train and eventually the locomotive with it. The full length of the train was 283ft. The line had been laid directly over the filled-in, 12ft diameter, 334yd deep No.7 New Zealand pit, part of the Low Hall Colliery group of eight shafts. This was situated half a mile east of Walthew Lane and a quarter of a mile north of Bickershaw Lane, Platt Bridge. The pit had closed in 1924 in its final years acting as a ventilation shaft. Filling of the shaft took place in 1931. Settlement then deterioration of the shaft lining led to a sudden collapse probably connected with regular shunting traffic passing over. The capped and refilled shaft today still contains Mr Berry along with the locomotive and wagons. Many people, including the family, feel Mr Berry's remains should be raised along with the locomotive, which could be displayed as a memorial both to him and the former workmen in the Wigan coalfields in general. A small memorial is in place at the site of the accident.

Low Hall Colliery *c*.1910. No.5 upcast pit is to the right, with its furnace ventilation chimney behind. No.6 downcast shaft is to the left. Moss Hall Coal Co. worked eight shafts altogether near Platt Bridge. An explosion on 15 November 1869 killed twenty-seven men and boys. The colliery closed when No.5 pit was abandoned in 1931.

Bamfurlong Colliery, 14 December 1892. A fire in the Pemberton Four Foot underground engine house led to sixteen men and boys being killed. The engine boy had made a paraffin rag torch to stop his compressed-air engine freezing, also pouring paraffin onto the cylinder and lighting it. This *Illustrated London News* engraving shows No.1 pit.

The Wigan Six Feet inset at Bamfurlong Colliery, c.1900. An official stands by as the onsetter raises the wooden gates and prepares to signal the cage to the surface. Two haulage hands shove in a couple of 6 or 7cwt tubs. At the time of the photograph they earned around £1.10 per week, colliers often only earning 10-50p extra. The colliery closed in 1936.

Office staff and management outside the Garswood Hall Colliery Company's offices, Wigan Road, Ashton In Makerfield, c.1906. At the time of the photograph the company was working ten different seams of coal from five shafts with 1,718 miners and 467 surface workers employed in total. Would you argue over your pay packet with the man on the right?

FIRE STATION

Garswood Hall Colliery No.5 (200yds pumping shaft) and No.6 (700yds, coal winding and ventilation) shafts, c.1958. Shafts were sunk in the area from the 1860s onwards. The colliery closed in 1958, its 655 miners and 163 surface workers transferring to nearby pits. Coal from other sites was washed here until 1962. The site is now the Three Sisters Country Park.

An explosion in the Ravine (Plodder) seam at Garswood Hall No.9 (Edge Green) pit killed twenty-seven men on 12 November 1932. Two more explosions occurred before Howe Bridge Rescue Team arrived. Here, a cage from the 400yd deep shaft has been blasted up into the wooden headgear. When this pit closed in 1938, 241 miners and forty-one surface workers lost their jobs.

In April 1959, twenty-one years after closure, the Garswood Hall No.9 shaft opened up due to the shaft filling slumping. No.9 pit had been sunk around 1905 to the Arley seam. The pit lay west of Edge Green Road, opposite the present day road tar works.

Park Colliery No.1, Garswood, *c*.1910, seen from No.2 pit. Main line wagons await loading from the screens, pit tubs visible on the gantry above. Pit props are stacked close to the shaft. The shaft sinking started in 1887, coal first arriving up No.1 in January 1888. J. and R. Stone owned the pit right up to nationalization of the industry in 1947, hence the local name 'Stones'.

This idyllic view of Park Colliery is from Liverpool Road looking north and dates from around the mid-1950s. From the right are Nos 1, 2 and 3 pits. Pithead baths, often only built in the 1930s, have escaped demolition after a number of Wigan area colliery closures. Those seen on the right still exist today as part of Park Industrial Estate.

Double drum Anderton Shearer Loader coalcutter at Park Colliery, 1957. This was developed by NCB engineers and fitters at Haydock workshops, then tested at Ravenhead Colliery, St Helens, in 1952 and at Golborne Colliery. The steel plough pushed cut coal onto the conveyor beneath. Park Colliery closed in June 1960, putting 350 miners and 108 surface employees out of work.

Smith & Sons owned Brynn Hall Colliery from 1856 until 1864, then Crippin and Smethurst from 1866 to 1893. Situated close to Park Brook Bridge, north of Bryn Gates Lane, this view from around.1945 has No.1 pit to the left and No.2 Pit on the right, sunk to the Arley seam at 430yds. Four hundred miners and 170 surface workers were employed when closure came in December 1945.

BRYNN HALL COLLIERY CO., Ltd.

Registered Office : Brynn Hall Collieries, near Wigan.
Telegraphic Address : " Brynn Hall Colliery, Bamfurlong, Wigan."
     Telephone No. : 7242 Ashton-in-Makerfield.

Directors : F. T. HANSON.
    T. W. BARKER.
    H. T. PIGOT.
Secretary : T. W. BARKER.

Name of Mine and Locality.	Manager.	Employees Under ground.	Above ground.	Railway and nearest Station.
Brynn Hall No. 2, Ashton	Robert Daniels	230	170	Brynn Hall Sidings.
Brynn Hall No. 3, Ashton		170		Bamfurlong

Seams Worked : Orrell Yard, Top Yard, 6 ft., Orrell 5 ft. L.M. **&** S.
Class of Coal : **Household, Gas, Manufacturing, Steam.**
Power Used : Steam, Compressed Air, Electricity, 3,300 and 550 volts.

Brynn Hall Colliery Co. in its final year in 1945, from the *Colliery Yearbook and Coal Trades Directory*. No self-respecting colliery manager would be without his copy, which listed all the coal mines, opencast sites, coal merchants, gasworks and associated industries and societies in Britain. The entry shows Nos 2 and 3 pits in production with four seams being worked, the coal being suitable for steam raising, gas production, household use and general industrial use. The former colliery site is now undergoing long-term restoration and landscaping work.

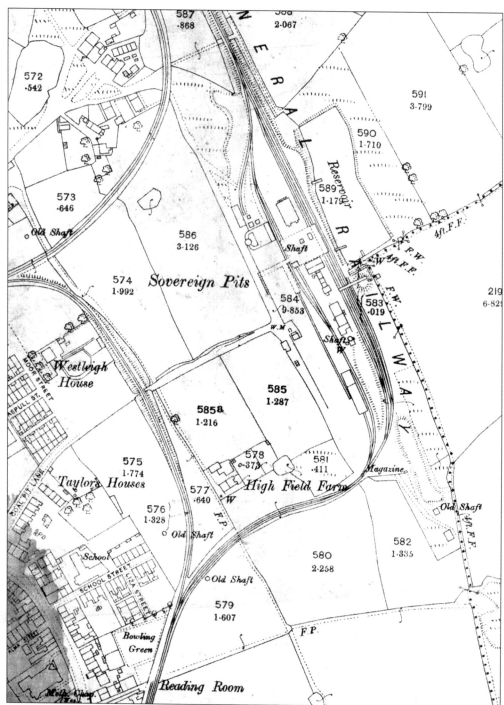

The 1892 25in OS plan, sheet 94.15 shows Sovereign Colliery at the end of Coal Pit Lane. The line to the north joined the LNWR near Howe Bridge West Junction. The plan only shows two shafts as No.3 was yet to be sunk (see photograph opposite). None of the colliery buildings remain today, the area having been landscaped.

Eight
Leigh and Golborne

Sovereign Pit, Pickley Green, Leigh, sunk in 1864 by Kirkless Hall Coal and Iron Company. Wigan Coal and Iron Co. took over in the early 1870s. Here in around 1908 are Nos 1, 2 and 3 pits from the north-west of Coal Pit Lane. No.1 Pit accessed the Arley seam at 649yds. The pit closed in December 1927; 301 miners and eighty-five surface workers had been employed.

Westleigh Colliery Co. Ltd, Lower Hall No.2, was half a mile south-east of Abram Colliery. Northeast were Westleigh Pit and Heyfield Pit. Lower Hall No.2 employed 174 miners and thirty-two surface workers in 1912 when the photograph was taken. A line linked the pits to Westleigh Canal Basin near Common Lane, Plank Lane. Lower Hall closed in 1918 and Heyfield in 1919.

Leigh Market Square during the 1926 strike. Henry Twist (1870-1934) speaks to local miners during the seven-month conflict. They were to be starved into accepting longer hours of work and a cut in wages. Born at Platt Bridge, Twist worked in mining from the age of eleven. Labour MP for Wigan 1910, Leigh 1922-1923. He was also an Executive Committee Member of the Mineworkers Federation, Great Britain in 1928 and Vice President of the Lancashire and Cheshire Mineworkers Federation from 1929-1934.

Bickershaw Colliery in 1887 from Greens Bridge on the Leeds & Liverpool Canal. This view comes from 'The Bickershaw Collieries', a booklet promoting the company's various coals. Note the canal-loading basin with gas lamp, also the stockpiled coal alongside No.1 pit. To the right from No.1 can be seen No.3 pit, No.2 pit and No.4 pit, all with wooden headgears.

This picture is entitled 'Ackers Whitley and Co. Ltd, Bickershaw Colliery, Leigh, winding engine 36" x 7' cylinders'. The 18ft diameter No.3 pit was sunk 650yds from 1877 to 1881, then to 779yds (the Plodder seam level) from 1933 to 1938. Here, in 1881, the new Walker Brothers of Wigan winder is in place, awaiting its rope. It was converted to electric winding in late 1977.

Bickershaw Colliery No.3 pit winding engine house after the overwind of 10 October 1932. The top cage, detached from the rope, was left hanging in the pit headgear. The winding rope and capel whipped over the pulley wheels and crashed through the engine house roof. The lower cage plunged into the sump at the pit bottom, drowning nineteen of the twenty miners inside.

'Leigh By The Sea', from around the 1930s. Subsidence from the 1870s onwards due to Bickershaw Colliery gradually created Leigh Flash. Regular flooding started in the late 1880s and moves to protect the area's wild birds began as early as 1906. By 1910 two farms had been lost to the Flash. Bickershaw Colliery last underworked the area in the Peacock seam in the 1980s.

When miner's helmets first arrived, men refused to pay a few pence for them! Bickershaw Colliery Co. issued helmets free of charge, often shared over three shifts. They had fittings for cap lamps but the men here at Bickershaw around 1937 are using electric 'bottle' hand lamps. The Safety in Mines Research Board advocated wider use of helmets after research in 1934.

The 779yd deep Bickershaw No.4 shaft in March 1939 during conversion to skip winding, the first such installation in the country. It was powered by a 2,500hp Metropolitan Vickers automatic electric winder still in use fifty years later. The aim was to wind forty-three times an hour, totalling 3,000 tons per seven-hour shift. This necessitated a winding speed of 43ft per second.

Five wooden headgears were in use at Bickershaw Colliery until 1952. No.5 was above a shaft only sunk in 1907-1908. This reached 305yds, accessing the Ince Yard seam. The shaft was deepened to 334yds in 1921 to reach the Crombouke seam. Later, the decision to take this shaft out of use and fill it was made, demolition taking place in 1952.

The famous Bickershaw Colliery Brass Band in 1956. The band was formed in 1919 as The Abram Colliery Prize Brass Band. In 1937, after reorganization of the company, the Bickershaw Colliery Band was formed. Major E. Hart MC became colliery manager in 1934, the band dominating his leisure time. After nationalization in 1947, he was badly treated by the NCB and, fearing for the future of the colliery and the band, he sadly became depressed, committing suicide in 1950.

No.1 Pit Bickershaw, in the mid-1960s. Time to remove one of the 16ft diameter pulley wheels. The pit was sunk in 1877 to 489yds and the original wooden headgear was replaced by this steel example from Abram Colliery in the late 1930s on formation of Bickershaw Collieries Ltd . It was wound for a century by a Woods of Wigan steam engine until conversion to electric in late 1977.

Bickershaw Colliery No.6, Brassey coalface worked under Leigh Flash in 1960. This photograph shows the 'waste' area left behind the face. Dowty hydraulic props and channel bars on the left redirected roof pressure away from the miner's working area. This allowed the waste area roof and strata above to collapse, leading to subsidence beneath the Flash.

Bickershaw Colliery featured the most impressive mining skyline the Lancashire coalfield has ever seen, with five headgears present until 1952. This view of 1970 from the south side of the Leeds & Liverpool Canal has, from left to right: Nos 1, 3, 2, and 4 Pits. In 1970 1,147 miners produced 593,000 tons of coal. The colliery's peak year was 1951 with 875,000 tons produced.

Bickershaw Colliery had steam locomotives in use as late as the early 1980s Here in June 1971 we see former Whitehaven coalfield locomotive *Respite*, a Hunslet 0-6-0 saddle tank of 1950, hauling a train of 21-ton coal wagons to exchange sidings at Abram. Parts of it were used to make the replica *Iron Duke* broad-gauge loco at the National Railway Museum in York.

A ranging drum shearer at work in the 8ft 4in-thick Rams seam, Bickershaw Colliery, around the late 1970s. The skills of experienced cuttermen such as George Buxton (in the photograph) to keep the faceline constant and avoid cutting into the rock floor or roof were often taken for granted. These men had to try to concentrate in very noisy, dusty and dangerous conditions.

This cheerful Bickershaw Colliery coalface team from around 1980 includes, from left to right: J.Coyle, -?-, Walter Flunt, Jack Sumner, 'Chopper', 'George', Ken Parker, Martin O'Rourke, Ken Greenall, Harry Gibson (Face Chargeman), 'Sil' Aspinall (Deputy) and A. Buckley. Face teams were kept together from face to face to ensure safety and efficiency.

Seams such as the Plodder contain large amounts of gas, released when worked, and at times in percentages which can be explosive. Here at Bickershaw Colliery around 1980, a methane drilling rig bores a drainage hole into another seam which might be 100ft above. Many holes were linked together to form a range, the gas then extracted and used on the surface.

Closure of Bickershaw Colliery had been announced when this photograph was taken in July 1992. Closest to the camera and bravely managing a smile is Frank Melia, the Surface Assistant Foreman Engineer. Highly skilled colliery engineers and fitters were adept at constructing to order and adapting equipment to suit specific coalface and underground conditions.

Portable 'self rescuers' based on First World War gas masks converted carbon monoxide to less toxic carbon dioxide. Here, at Albert Colliery (1939-1965) near Bickershaw in 1963, a miner is shown the correct way to wear his 'dustbin' type rescuer. In the event of a fire or explosion this gave the man up to half an hour to get to a fresh air base.

Time for a break for these cheerful women surface workers from Parsonage Colliery, Leigh, in 1925. Behind them stands a twelve-ton Wigan Coal and Iron Co. wagon. Their uniform of clogs, stout stockings, dust apron and shawl seem identical to those worn sixty years earlier. Nearly fifty were employed at Parsonage in 1925. Women's baths were not provided until 1933.

A backdrop of private owner coal wagons, the one to the right originating from Amalgamated Anthracite Collieries in South Wales, sets the scene as pre-nationalization. Possibly all of Parsonage Colliery's forty-five women surface workers are in this wartime photograph of 1940.

Parsonage Colliery, c.1956 from the Wigan Road end of Sportsmans Street. The colliery line (disused at the time of the photograph) crossed Twist Lane, heading towards Springfield Canal Basin. The man walking home overcoat in hand, the gas lamp on the street corner, the child on a tricycle, no TV aerials…it all brings back happy memories for us forty-somethings!

A late 1960s view of Parsonage Colliery No.1 steam winder, installed in 1923, three years after shaft sinking was completed to 1,007yds. By Galloways of Manchester and rated at 3,000hp, the engine's cylinders of 40in diameter by 6ft stroke wound a drum which varied from 16ft to 22ft in diameter. The colliery's peak output was 517,000 tons in 1968-1969, with 747 miners on the books.

Parsonage Colliery, 1979. Water bottles had long been a necessity with strata temperatures of 118°F in the 4,000ft-deep Arley seam workings. In the late 1920s and early 1930s, men took seven pint cans of water on shift. Salt water was supplied to replace losses due to sweating. A man could also expect to lose 7lb in weight each day, putting 4lb back on at night!

Parsonage No.2 downcast shaft headgear was demolished, not without a struggle, on 30 September 1992. Sinking by Wigan Coal and Iron Co. started in June 1913, before progress was halted in January 1914, the First World War delaying operations for two years. The Arley seam, at 998yds, was eventually reached in late 1920. Nos 1 and 2 pits were for many years the deepest shafts in Britain. No.2 was an early example of a ferro-concrete structure of immense strength to withstand coal winding from over 980yds, the two-deck cage taking 8 x 10 cwt tubs. With a 2in diameter winding rope of 225 tons breaking strain passing over 18ft diameter pulleys, it was wound by a Markhams of Chesterfield 4,000hp steam engine. An electric GEC 2,200hp installation replaced steam power in 1978. Coal winding ceased in 1983-1984 when Bickershaw Colliery became the main outlet for the Bickershaw-Parsonage-Golborne Complex.

Previous pages: If the roadway sides were strong but the roof was weak, 'cockering' or herringbone timbering was used. Parsonage Colliery had a good example of cockering dating back to the late 1930s in the Bickershaw 7ft seam. Photographed in April 1992 after the colliery had closed, many old documents, signs and objects were rescued from these workings before being sealed off.

Miners and their families from Bickershaw, Parsonage and Golborne collieries resigned to closure of the Complex, made a final proud gesture on 27 March 1992. They marched from Bickershaw Colliery to Leigh Miners Welfare, Plank Lane. Many a tear was shed by older onlookers who saw this as the end of an era which had given character to the community, a community that had been particularly badly treated by a uniquely uncaring government. The hundreds of miners who died at local pits were especially remembered. Parsonage Colliery awaits demolition in the background – a Sainsburys supermarket is now in its place.

Old Bedford Colliery, east of Lilford Woods, had been in production in the 1830s. Nos 1 and 2 Pits (431 and 617yds), seen here in around 1910, were sunk by John Speakman in 1874. An explosion on Friday August 13 1886 killed thirty-eight men and boys. No.3 Pit was sunk in 1916 to the Arley seam at 766yd. This view from the west looks across the LNWR Tyldesley-Leigh railway line.

Bedford Colliery's original owner, John Speakman, died in 1873, his name living on in John Speakman & Sons Ltd from 1914 until March 1929, when the company became part of Manchester Collieries Ltd. This photograph of December 1937 shows the new pithead baths for 900 men and fifty-six women. A grant of £18,000 came from the Miners Welfare Fund.

The women's section of the new pithead baths at Bedford Colliery provided for fifty-six screen workers. This photograph of December 1937 shows women in the rest room attached to their baths. The description in the Miners Welfare Fund Report stated that: '…this rest room often becomes the centre of welfare activity which extends beyond the hours of work.'

Night shift cutterman and faceworker at Bedford Colliery, c.1942. From 1936 to 1945, the percentage of coal cut by machines in the Manchester Collieries pits rose from 37% to 96%. This machine undercut the coalface ready for shotholes to be drilled. Coal blasted down was hand-loaded onto the conveyor belt on the early shift (around 7 a.m. to 2 p.m.) the next day.

Coal driller using a Power Vane compressed-air drill at Bedford Colliery, 1942. In a seven-hour shift a driller might drill 100 holes along the faceline, each four feet deep. Here the seam has a dirt or shale band high up (near the miner's head) which was cut and removed before firing the coal. This was a hard, dusty and noisy job, yet skilled – it was important that it was carried out correctly.

Bedford Colliery, 1942. Faceworkers setting a metal friction prop or 'finger trapper' beneath a corrugated channel bar. These men worked a 'ratch' or 'braid' as much as 25 metres long, hand-filling the coal which had been blasted down, building roof-support stone packs, and advancing all the props and bars. It was an arduous job which only strong, fit men could manage.

Bedford Colliery, 1954. The central conveyor tunnel midway along the coalface. Temporary timber supports are set against the stone 'ripping lip'. This has to be brought down and new steel arch girders set. Bedford closed in October 1967 due to exhaustion of reserves and working close to a built up area. This meant unemployment for 581 miners and 131 surface workers.

Nos 2, 1, and 3 pits, Golborne Colliery, seen from Church Street in 1927, from *Romance of Coal* by Richard Evans & Co. The sinking of Nos 1 and 2 was begun in 1878 by Edward Johnson, owner of Swan Lane and Long Lane Collieries. Richard Evans & Co. of Haydock purchased the pit in 1880, when winding commenced. In 1890 No.3 was sunk to the Trencherbone.

Golborne Colliery, July 1961. This picture shows the fallen 'waste' behind the line of hydraulic roof supports on the Trencherbone rise coalface. The rock above this seam contained freshwater mussel fossils and often sheared off in a straight line as in the photograph, at times over a wide area – not the nicest of surprises when it had been hanging for weeks! Note the cutter marks in the roof.

Golborne Colliery Nos 2 and 3 from the south-east in the early 1970s. To access unworked reserves of coal it was decided to link Golborne via tunnels to Bickershaw Colliery in 1975-1976. Sadly the 1970s also brought the Golborne Disaster of 18 March 1979, when ten men died in the Plodder district after an explosion of methane. The colliery closed in 1989.

Golborne had for most of its life been a very productive and efficient colliery. Here in 1986, three years before closure, state-of-the-art underground transport methods are in use, namely Free Steered Vehicles. Depending on the nature of the floor these could transport heavy materials along roadways without the need for rails or haulage engines.

Nine
Atherton and Tyldesley

Howe Bridge, Atherton, model mining village from the west, photographed in 1980 from the temporary bridge for the opencast site at Millers Lane. Built in 1875 mainly for Gibfield Arley miners, the village is probably a unique survivor of its type and certainly the most impressive in the country. A few years ago it was designated a conservation area and will now hopefully survive insensitive development. The raised walkway on the left was and still is known as 'The Prom', or promenade. The village of two-up, two-down cottages was laid out to the designs of Medland Taylor. Colliery owners Fletcher Burrows and Company included shops, public baths, an infants and junior school and a village club and contributed towards the building of St Michaels church. Atherton Collieries Joint Association was formed in 1918, the cricket ground coming under its wing as well as two tennis courts, a bowling green and the village club. In 1921 the Coffee Pot Club opposite Atherton Town Hall was opened for the men. Here they could play cards, dominoes, snooker and billiards and hold other meetings as varied as debating and drama societies. Wives and daughters of Fletcher Burrows' miners could even find employment at the company's Howe Bridge Mills. Howe Bridge was in every way a model mining community. Fletcher Burrows and Co. considered every need, including leisure, education, health and spiritual needs. They also made sure conditions below ground were as safe as possible and for many years were the leaders nationally in safe working practices. The author spent some of the happiest years of his life at Howe Bridge School, which even today is held in high regard.

The 1893 strike. Miners and families at Howe Bridge Colliery search for coal. The single wheel headgear of Lovers Lane Colliery (closed 1898) is behind the pit to the far left. Howe Bridge's

unusual wooden headgear of 1879, giving it the nickname 'Bicycle Pit', survived until closure in 1959. The furnace ventilation chimney above the Volunteer shaft is on the right.

The Minimum Wage Strike of February to April 1912 brought out the whole of Britain's coalmining workforce, over one million miners. After the experience of 1893, food kitchens were set up in Atherton, as here at Chowbent School. A mob of 800 non-local miners rioted near Chanters Colliery at the end of the strike, resulting in the 16th Hussars being called out from Wigan.

Edward Ormerod (1834-1894), centre, displaying his range of safety winding detaching hooks at his Gibfield Colliery, Atherton, works, c.1890. Patented in 1868, they detached the winding rope from the cage if overwound, after passing through the iron 'bell'. They were first tested in 1867, with Ormerod insisting on being alone in the cage, and are now used in mines worldwide.

Lovers Lane, Atherton, c.1910. On the left, the first central mines rescue training station in the country opened in 1908. Set up by The Lancashire and Cheshire Coalowners Association, it was soon required by the Maypole, Abram disaster in August of that year. Closed in November 1933 after the opening of Boothstown Mines Rescue Station with its permanent rescue corps.

The disaster of 21 December 1910 at Pretoria Colliery, over Hulton, near Atherton, resulted in the deaths of 344 men and boys. Howe Bridge had by then trained over 200 men from the north-west, including these men seen from around 1911. Instructor Sergeant Major W.H. Hill is third from the right, William Ewins, first from the right. Note the Proto breathing apparatus, electric lamps and canary cage.

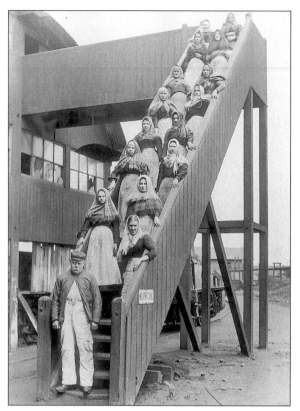

In 1905 a series of photographs were taken for Fletcher Burrows of their Atherton Collieries. Here at Howe Bridge, colliery women screen workers along with their foreman patiently pose. Lantern slides were made which Clement Fletcher occasionally showed to interested groups. Female screen workers had left Howe Bridge by the early 1950s.

Another of the 1905 Fletcher Burrows Atherton Collieries series, this time taken at Gibfield Colliery. Just for once the pit brow girls are laughing, and with every reason, because if you look very closely at the second row they are in fact men dressed up as women to fill up the numbers!

Viewed in 1905 from the Bolton to Leigh railway line of 1828 is Gibfield Colliery No.1 Arley Pit. Sunk 400yds in 1872 it replaced Old Gib Pit of 1829. No.2 Pit of 410yds served for ventilation. Loco Atherton, a 0-4-0 well tank by Hawthorns of Leith was purchased in 1867. The coal washery behind, of 1892, was one of the first in the country.

Chanters Colliery No.1 Pit, 1905. This colliery lay south of Tyldesley Old Road, near Hindsford, now Chanters industrial estate. It was close to the site of very old shafts dating back to the late seventeenth century. The men here have finished work and will soon be in the showers. Note the water cans, flat caps and the boy's long clog soles for sliding down rails.

Gibfield Colliery lamp room, 1905. Miners at Atherton Collieries had oil safety lamps provided for them. The lamp man dismantled the lamps, checked their internal gauzes and wicks, cleaned, refilled and relit them. They provided about one candlepower of light and indicated the prescence of gas or lack of oxygen. Clay pipes and food tins can be seen on the racks.

Chanters No.1 Pit stands behind this crowd at Hindsford Bridge on 11 April 1912. The Minimum Wage Strike from February to April saw rioting, mainly by outsiders, in Atherton, especially on 10 April. At the time of this photograph the 16th Hussars from Wigan and local police had ensured men could return to work without danger.

After a trial installation at Howe Bridge Colliery in 1912, Gibfield Colliery baths – the first in the country – opened on 15 September 1913 with a capacity of 400. Seen here in late 1913, continental practice was put into use with numbered clothes hangers enabling overnight drying of wet work clothes. The building still stands today as a warehouse.

Captioned 'Before And After', this photograph of late 1913 shows a young lad resplendent in huge flat cap, waistcoat and scarf after his shower at Gibfield baths. To his left is an example of 'the unwashed'. This was one of a series of photographs of Gibfield baths, where in every one the young boy's eyes are firmly closed!

An early example of aerial photography gives a glimpse of Howe Bridge Colliery from the south. Taken around 1925, this shows the Bolton to Leigh railway line heading north-east to Gibfield Colliery a mile away. The chimney is close to the Victoria Pit headgear, the tall white building to its right being the old vertical engine house for the Puffer Pit pumping shaft.

Locomotives *Gordon* (left) and *Crawford* (right) at Howe Bridge in the early 1960s. *Gordon* was an 0-6-0ST of 1945 by Stephenson and Hawthorns, at Chanters by 1946 and there until its closure in 1966. *Crawford* was an ex-Wigan Coal and Iron Co.-built 0-6-0ST sent to Gibfield Colliery in 1957 from NCB Kirkless workshops. Scrapped at Gibfield in 1964 soon after the pit closed.

The training gallery at Howe Bridge Rescue Station in late 1920s. A brigade of men from a north-west colliery is on a refresher course, working in full breathing apparatus to place a miner into a metal stretcher. On training exercises rescuemen were forced to exert themselves as close as possible to the level they would expect in an incident.

Locomotive *Ellesmere*, seen at Howe Bridge Colliery shortly before removal to a Scottish railway museum in September 1957. Made by Hawthorns of Leith in 1861, its name was later changed to 1861 to avoid confusion with one of the Bridgewater Collieries' stock. The cut away cab allowed for travelling the tunnel to Bedford Basin, Leigh, on the Bridgewater Canal.

Howe Bridge Colliery from the south-west, on closure in September 1959, when 242 miners and forty-two surface workers were employed. Two shafts were sunk by John Fletcher and others in 1850, 150yds to the Brassey, Rams and Seven Feet seams. A surface drift to the Crombouke and Brassey also worked from 1870 to 1907. After nationalization in 1947, the average output was 130,000 tons. Prince Philip paid the pit's Area Training Centre a visit in 1952.

The coalface, Chanters Colliery No1 Pit, 1929, probably in the Yard seam. The face is to the left, working to the rise. A tub awaits filling and sending down the 'jig brow' gravity incline, via the square metal skid plate. This picture was taken to show new metal friction props in place of wooden ones. Safety was a priority at Fletcher Burrows' pits, often found at the top of the area's leagues.

Chanters Colliery No.2 Pit, *c*.1925. The winding engine man rests on the crosshead of the Greenhalgh and Co. engine. Greenhalgh's had their works near present day Lifting Gear Hire on Bolton Road, Atherton. Some of the buildings still stand. Erected in 1896 the engine raised three tons from a depth of 600yds and was in use until the colliery closed in June 1966.

Below ground, Chanters Colliery No.1 Pit, 1944. This was William Hughes' (right) twenty-seventh and last year as undermanager. He deputized for the pit manager, controlling all aspects of work below ground. William started at Chanters in 1893, when horses were used for haulage. He also had twenty years service on the rescue team, including attending the Pretoria Disaster in 1910.

Black faced mineworkers having a brew at Gibfield Colliery canteen on 29 May 1947. In the back of their minds perhaps, now the colliery was nationalized, was what lay ahead. Apparently nationalization made little difference to working practices for most men at Atherton Collieries who had in general been well treated by Fletcher Burrows and Co.

Atherton Photographic Society meeting down the Tyldesley Old Road, Atherton, c.1955. On the horizon is Chanters No.2 Pit, sunk in 1850 and later deepened to 600yds. The colliery raised 427,214 tons in 1955. Many old shallow shafts, including one containing seventeenth-century coins, existed here. Closed in 1966, most of the 1,059 miners and 284 surface workers were relocated.

August 1963. Gibfield Colliery's 725 miners and 116 surface workers have lost their jobs. The offices (left) and lamp room are seen from Coal Pit Lane. Late eighteenth-century shafts already existed here when George Stephenson's Bolton to Leigh Railway opened in 1828. As a wartime safety measure, Gibfield Colliery was connected below ground to Chanters Colliery.

Astley Green Colliery, April 1909. Temporary wooden sinking headgears stand above No.1 and No.2 Pits. These were sunk by Pilkington Colliery Co. Ltd, a branch of Clifton & Kersley Coal Co. Ltd. Boreholes predicted that sinking would be difficult due to watered drift deposits. A cast iron 'tubbing ring' circle with cutting edge had to be forced through the loose ground by jacks.

Head Wrightson and Co. building the 80ft high steel headgear at Astley Green No.1 Pit in April 1911. The 15ft high brick pillar, metal collar and twelve hydraulic rams weighed 2,200 tons, countering the thrust as the steel cutting ring and tubbing was forced downwards. The 21ft diameter shaft reached 890yds in 1912. Note the sinking headgear still inside the new one.

Yates and Thom's workmen in front of No.1 Pit's 109-ton winding drum, September 1911. The 3,300hp engine ordered for Astley Green from the Blackburn company was of such a size due to expectations of large outputs from unfaulted ground to the south. This was around the period of peak output in Britain's coal mines, with 287 million tons raised in 1913.

MAY 9TH 1916

Astley Green No.2 Pit was sunk to 833yds with a 21ft diameter like No.1 Pit. Due to the First World War, construction of the steel headgear was delayed until 1916. Here in May of that year the 18ft diameter pulley is ready for hoisting into place. The wooden sinking headgear can be seen behind. The Yates and Thom steam winder for No.2 came into use during 1919.

Astley Green No.1 Pit, *c.*1915. Winding engine man Mr Roscoe in control of one of the largest colliery steam winding engines ever seen in the world, the 500-ton Yates and Thom of Blackburn 3,300hp, four-cylinder, twin tandem compound. Ten years after closure the Red Rose Live Steam Society began restoring the engine, creating the nucleus for a future museum.

Astley Green No.2 Pit Yates and Thom winding engine. This was similar in detail to No.1 engine but was a single-sided, horizontal, cross compound version, with two cylinders of 36in and 60in diameter and 72in stroke. It was converted to six-ton skip winding in 1947. Winding at the time of the photograph (the early 1960s), was from the Worsley seam at 283yds. Note the depth indicator dial.

The end of a gruelling seven-and-a-half-hour shift down Astley Green Colliery, October 1934. The men and boys have just come up No.1 Pit, with No.2 Pit towering in the distance. Oldham's electric 'bottle' lamps are being carried. These gave illumination of up to three candlepower compared with a miner's oil lamp which might manage a half to one candlepower. The trouble was that miners still needed an oil lamp to test for gas or low oxygen and the electric lamp weighed nearly ten pounds. In 1934, earnings at Astley Green were amongst the highest in the country for the 1,300 miners and 450 surface workers.

An atmospheric scene at Astley Green Colliery, *c*.1933. It's payday and the temptation of the Ross's Arms is only a few yards away! Towering behind is No.1 Pit, still standing today and the only surviving colliery headgear in the Lancashire Coalfield. It is also the finest example left in the country. Pithead baths and canteen were to be built on the left by 1936.

Astley Green Colliery, around the late 1940s. A mineral tramroad had existed from Tyldesley Coal Company's Yew Tree Colliery down to the Leeds & Liverpool Canal at Astley as far back as the mid 1850s. Clifton and Kersley Coal Co. purchased the sidings and tippler in 1913. Bickershaw Colliery, Leigh, was the last to use the canal for coal transport, finishing in August 1972.

At the coalface, Astley Green colliery, 1942. A young miner begins to shovel dirt into the middle of the stone pack he is building on the left. Stone and dirt packs were spaced out every few yards along the face, taking roof pressure away from the coalface and sending it towards the waste area. This face must have been cool for a change as he still has his shirt on!

A happy group of screens women at Astley Green Colliery. Women worked on the screens at Astley until August 1955, the date of the photograph. The job was a dirty and dusty one. Working in the screen sheds in winter could be pretty harsh, yet, as with those who worked underground, the camaraderie of working with others made it bearable.

Men from the last shift at Astley Green Colliery, April 1970. Parkside, Bickershaw and Parsonage pits accepted most of the 1,192 miners. Eight years before closure a life of fifty to eighty years had been forecast by the NCB. Closure of all the pits to the north left a mounting water burden on the pit, with constant pressure by the NCB to achieve unrealistic output targets.

Nook Colliery Nos 4, 3, 1 and 2 Pits Tyldesley, c.1936. No.5 Jubilee Pit is out of view. Shaft sinking began in 1864 and by 1913 No.4 Arley pit (left) had been sunk by Astley and Tyldesley Coal and Salt Co. Ltd to 944yds, intersecting nineteen workable seams. Temperatures in the Arley workings reached 100°F, resulting in men having to take salt tablets and working virtually naked.

Nook Colliery pithead baths, canteen and cycle store from the south-west after opening on 24 April 1937. Costing £23,000 and funded by the Miners Welfare Fund and Manchester Collieries Ltd, this accomodated 2,000 men and seventy-six female surface workers. Men contributed 3d per week towards running costs. The building is still standing today as premises for a small business.

Nook Colliery, No.4 Arley level in 1948. A welcome but definitely third class ride of over a mile from the coalface to the pit bottom. The manriding train is being hauled by a flameproof diesel locomotive, one of the first to be installed at a north-west colliery. Capable of 12mph, with a maximum gradient of 1 in 20, it was one of 150 ordered by the NCB at the time.

Nook Colliery pit bus in the lodge, 3 August 1950, with No.4 Arley Pit behind. The LUT bus had started back after dropping off sixty miners, hit the kerb, lost control and crashed through the lodge railings. Miner Fred Canning and others ran back, diving in to rescue unconscious driver Harold Sydall from the submerged cab. The conductress had managed to jump off.

Two old headgears, one steel, the other wood, at Combermere Colliery, Combermere Lane, Tyldesley, in the early 1960s. This was a Tyldesley Colliery Co. mine sunk around the 1860s to the Rams seam at 100yds. After closure in 1903, it was used as a brickworks until the late 1950s, then to wind water in a tank cage for the lodges at Cleworth Hall Colliery to the south-east.

Wharton Hall Colliery No.2 Pit engine house and headgear from the east in the early 1960s. Sunk 550yds to the Arley seam around the mid-1860s by Francis Charlton. Northeast of Combermere Colliery, the pit later came under the Trustees of the Duke of Bridgewater. It was a pumping station from 1928 until 1965, and linked to Brackley and Ashton's Fields Collieries.

A real family affair on't rucks at Cleworth Hall Colliery, Tyldesley during the 1926 strike. Old tips in the 1920s contained plenty of small coal due to inefficient washing. Fatalities occurred in most coalfields as outcroppers were buried under collapses. No-one needed a weather vane in Tyldesley due to the sulphur fumes given off by this burning tip for generations!

Fred Norris, aged thirty-six, Cleworth Hall Colliery oiler and greaser and Olympic 10,000 metres athlete, receives a framed colour print of himself from workmates in May 1959. He was the first Briton to cover more than twelve miles in one hour, a record only Heino and Zatopek could equal. One of Britain's finest long-distance runners, his achievements are far too numerous to list here.

Cleworth Hall Colliery after closure in January 1963. East of Tyldesley and north of Manchester Road, this was sunk by Tyldesley Coal Co. Ltd in the early 1870s. The Arley was later to be reached at 662yds. This view looking east is of No.3 (front) and No.2 Pits. In its final year, 554 miners and 117 surface workers produced 113,911 tons of coal.

This picture was taken in the Tyldesley area, possibly at Cleworth Hall Colliery, in the late 1930s. The miner is in charge of a compressed-air Siskol coal cutter, nicknamed a 'chomper' due to its rotary and hammer action. The drill is anchored between roof and floor while cutting out a dirt band. Wood 'nogs' were then wedged in the cut until time for hand coal loading.

Looking north across the fields towards Mort Lane, Tyldesley in the early 1940s, we see New Lester Colliery. The original owner around 1867 was James Roscoe. Deepened in the mid-1890s, 535yds to the Arley seam, an unexpected bonus was the 1ft 8in Denner Main seam at 400yds. The colliery had ceased coal production by 1944. It is now a general industrial site.

Tyldesley Local Defence Volunteers march proudly past Leigh MP Joe Tinker (left) in the field near Gin Pit Miners Welfare in the summer of 1940. This was followed up by an inspection of the ATC at St Georges Colliery behind. There are few existing photographs of St Georges Colliery, with its distinctive wooden water cooling tower, facing pit headgears and 180ft high chimney. St George's church stands behind.

St Georges Colliery No.2 upcast shaft and fan chimney after closure in 1964. Locally known as 'Back O't Church Pit'. Two shafts sunk in 1866 to the Rams seam were later enlarged and deepened to the Arley at 786yds. The colliery ceased coal winding in 1941. In its final years it served as a training centre for miners.

Ten
A Coalopolis Miscellany

Wigan Cannel coal is an amazing material, formed from the deposition of lake sediments such as algae. It is hard and dense, feeling rather like Bakelite to the touch. With care it could be worked, turned and polished as with this urn of around 1880 promoting Wigan Coal and Iron Co. Visitors to 'Coalopolis' from the early eighteenth century onwards could purchase items crafted by local artisans. Some fine examples have survived in Wigan's Department of Heritage collections.

Moves to ban women from surface work at pits in 1887 led to a deputation to the Home Secretary of Lancashire pit women, successfully blocking legislation. 'Pit Brow Lasses at Work' is an oil by Manchester artist Arthur Wasse probably showing Mesnes Colliery, Frog Lane Wigan. Commissioned by Wigan mineowners for the Library Street Mining College, it was first exhibited at the Royal Academy in 1887, Chicago in 1936 and Paris in 1955.

Some Wigan miners kept occupied during the 1921 strike by flying their pigeons. The man on the left is noting the time the bird is released. The miner's love of nature goes back to the earliest days. Underground, he was deprived of other life forms apart from men, mice, ponies and rats. This enhanced his appreciation for the things people on the surface took for granted.

No doubting the outcome of this vote in Wigan Market Square six days before the 1921 strike began on 1 April! The economic slump in the coal industry after years of wartime government control had brought a drop in prices. The coal owners announced a 50% cut in wages, while the men withdrew their labour and were 'locked out' from returning.

The 1921 strike or lockout, Wigan. This lasted three months but was not able to counter a 20% drop in wages. Sat on their clog heels as they would below ground at the coalface, men would chat for hours on end, then perhaps head off to the fields for a game of cards, race the dogs or even have a fight, all for money of course!

Many a Wigan area coal miner would have seen this NCB safety poster in the late 1950s. Pinned up either in the lamp room or near the man-riding train sidings at pit bottom, this put an important message over in ways he would recognize! There is a saying that holds true in former mining areas: 'More coal has been mined in the taproom than ever below ground.'

Known as 'The Three Sisters' or 'The Wigan Alps,' this 1960s landscape was created by Mains Colliery and others tipping washery and screens waste. A great playground for children – sliding down the sides on cardboard boxes was my favourite! Hidden dangers included burning cavities emitting sulphurous gas and slurry ponds full of 'sinky slutch'!